ALIEN
PHONICS
PRIMER

POEMS BY
DARRELL EPP

First Edition

Cover image by Keith Giles
Cover design by Matthew J. Distefano
Interior layout by Matthew J. Distefano

ISBN 978-1-964252-08-7

Printed in the United States of America

 QUOIR

Published by Quoir
Chico, California
www.quoir.com

CONTENTS

Also by Darrell Epp

"I believe I undertook amongst other things not to disclose any trade secrets. Well, I am not going to."

— Joseph Conrad

The Western Wind

download self-help pdf's, draw a plan, a map,
mutant stick-man power rangers, bible battle
scenes with transhuman color schemes,
end up somehow neck-deep inside the
jasmine bush, gakked-out and speeding
on the excruciating sweetness of it all:
this explains how i missed the bus, the
ladder of success just firewood now, and
my graduating class voted me most likely
to stop reading before the end of the
sentence. and who needs a car anyhow,
when wind is free and i can stretch out
my wings and catch a westward breeze?
it's even easier down by cootes paradise
marsh, with wind whipping off the lake
and the old lift bridge—conscripted into
the nafta superhighway—groaning under
the weight of gdp-boosting supertankers.
but even parliamentarians must bow to
the transcendental—i cheered when the
buckthorn and prickly ash popped holes
in all their grand plans. the future is ours.
here comes that western wind again:
fog-etched grace notes hitch a ride.

Quantum Legend

a man howls at the urinal, slaps his palm against
the tile. if this was a legend he'd know what path
to choose, and just up ahead a mighty horse and
a magic key. a princess would ask, going my way?
and why does time slow down when you're waiting,
like a scream in a dream that's really your darth
vader alarm clock, another second and you'd have
had it all: a rope tethered to her heart, an immovable
rock, the garlic, the yogurt, the shopping list you
lost and how it haunted you, that look in her eyes.
the quantum field we're all falling through leaves
lint on my sweater and moldy bread in the toaster.
reality comes with some assembly required and
disloyal dice. tim plays the record backwards,
looking for hidden messages. lys turns the sheet
music upside down, doesn't miss a beat, andante,
allegro, notes rising into the smoke, vanishing like
stale clues. question marks bloomed in my mind
while i stared at the sky until my mind became
the sky. keeping it all straight's like lunging from
trapeze to trapeze, or dancing on a volcano
in a summer blockbuster, the one the oscar
voters ignored. opening doors with a bloody
forehead was always my plan a. sure it hurts.

That's Not a Piñata, That's a Hornets' Nest

there's a war on, i mean negotiations have
broken down between the natural world
and the tonka toy dump trucks. steel-belted
giant wheels ran over a butterfly and don't
ask me why i'm screaming—why aren't you?
a secret wish, slammed into the boards;
the leaves of the paper birch, sandwiched
between a dying neuron and a cruel future.
martin buys a new shovel, says there's a
civilization below the one below this one
where angels never get tangled in power
lines, and there's a talking book guiding
all the runaways home, and kites ascend
forever. so start digging! over here, there's a
squid that changes color when it's dreaming,
labor unrest at the thunderbolt factory, and
whispered hints of weightlessness between
system updates. my first gold star equals
the unpopped popcorn at the bottom of the
bag, so says ebay and facebook marketplace.
isn't it wild, just guessing on multiple-choice
tests, watching the wolves until the sun is
gone and you can't even tell whose carcass
they're dividing? this town was made for me.

Dreaming Without a Helmet

knock-knock, says the naughty memory lurking
one inch behind my forehead. who is it, says
my prehistoric reptile brain, don't make me
come up there. tired of juggling my unruly
thought parade, my spinal column sits down
on an ikea futon made in sweden where they
take the dance of form and function seriously.
st. patrick's bell rings out, reminding me that
i haven't felt guilty for one whole hour. i start
over, reset the timer, bump into a cosmologist
who says most of reality is missing. i say it's
not missing, it's hiding, we split the difference,
share an uber, a membrane of memory haunts
the collector lane like a half-heard riddle. equation
without a constant, see-saw sunset no one saw,
glittering cloud-shroud in need of a tune-up. the
mint gave a billion dollar bills to the haves, told
the have-nots to pray harder. dreaming without
a helmet is dangerous but so is air in ward 3 in
the city of industry. there's a post-it note on the
fridge that says, my thoughts are not me and i
am a stranger to myself. i don't recognize the
handwriting. my hand points at the moon; i
stare at my hand. some weeks last a year.

Parachutist Impaled on Rhino Horn

the house of frankenstein's been remodeled past
all recognition: fake sand on a fake beach chokes
the native topsoil. security reprimanded me for
crying in front of the tourists, but what else could
i do when they replaced our first dairy queen with
an inflatable giant hand advertising luxury condos?
parachutist impaled on rhino horn crawls across the
bottom of the screen and the family dog leaves us
for a scuba diver with an open-top jeep. the midnight
laundromats i haunted. the caterpillar i trapped in a
bottle, then forgot to feed. is this part of the gag? the
sad clown asks the by-law enforcement officer. how
will i know when you're about to let go? the plum asks
the branch. when in doubt i always checked off all of
the above, stuffed my pockets with free packets of
butter at the mandarin buffet. the thing about high
school is picking the right locker. the thing about
funerals is there are too many of them. today i
confused canada with a jigsaw puzzle dropped
from a great height. a cartoon coyote hangs in
the air, silently asks the cruel camera for mercy.
melanie hits me with a flower, i pretend it doesn't
hurt; most of the bleeding's internal anyway. the
joker couldn't stop laughing even if he wanted to.

The Law of Erosion

what doth the new terms and conditions require of
thee? even when i stab the dart right into the
bullseye, the target's my own twilight zone reflection.
hope is the thing with feathers, not the tyrant building
his pyramid with slave labor, not the suitcase full of
monopoly money left behind in the motel 6. without
feathers we'd be so naked we might stare at our
phones all day just to avoid the shame. at last comes
the bafflement, but hark, it also comes first: the dr.'s
slap, the tears, and the downhill slide. try to learn
something before rigor mortis sets in; it all flashes
by the passenger window so quickly. the specialist
leaned back in his chair, said there were some
challenges we had to face on the road ahead.
back then i was always falling in love with random
strangers. the tragedy isn't falling, it's falling from
an insufficiently majestic mountain. should have
studied the law of erosion before building my
monument out of dust. a shoe is lost, a word
falls out of common usage and that's not a
pothole, that's an impact crater. the first week
i said her name a thousand times. o traitorous
mirror in the white of the eye! o stolen walmart
shopping cart, brimming over with doll parts!

Win a Dream Date with Queen Amnesia

even changing shirts makes me feel like a tourist,
and when it comes to picking locks i'm all thumbs.
here's the thing about gutted victorian houses,
here's the thing about souls. and isn't it cruel,
the vicious lottery that decides which meme
lives and which one dies. a hasty rewrite that
would have redeemed everything, lost at sea.
i saw the strong erotic force grind concrete into
powder and electrons colliding like bumper cars
behind my third eye. i remember punches thrown,
and salty tears, but not quite the why of it all.
there are no admirals on the river of forgetfulness.
to blind queen amnesia, we're all commoners
in a bumbling democracy of slapstick shadows.
there are halos in her retinas, galaxies you can't
touch without a stepladder and gooseberry
bushes barely resisting the urge to catch fire
and fly away. taproots tickle the world's iron core.
this leaf really is something. i bet if i stare at it
long enough, this leaf will turn into a prism.
it really is a wonder how so few of our thoughts
bloom into action. once i sprained my ankle to
avoid stepping on a snail. once there was
an ice cream truck i thought was a dragon.

The Teardrop Collector Appreciates Your Business

a pinecone hits the ground with a baleful thud
and suddenly i wish i was wearing a tuxedo.
gurinder's cat plays with a discarded coke can.
attic dormers leer at us like jack-o-lanterns.
as the worm chews through the calendar,
cruel time drops the cosmetic camouflage.
this is what you want: this is what you get.
dear big bang, let me talk to your manager,
preferably sometime before this ashy soil
and the ash i'm made out of are terminally
reunited. and where have all the inventors
gone? there used to be crackpots with flying
machines lined up around the block, just
waiting for the patent office to open. if cold
fusion's out, how about a bloom that never
fades? but i know i've always been greedy,
my very first word was 'more.' selena says
calm down but i'm not calm as i find myself
second-guessing ifrah's old address and
wouldn't it be nice if, at the end of time,
there was someone who could find all the
things we lost, turn our poisoned utopias
into zen gardens? atoms from the sun
like angels on parole boil away my tears.

Piano with a Flat Tire

so many sublets with fist- and boot-shaped holes in
the drywall: back then we didn't need the internet
to have a good time. after a billion birthdays,
how can clocks on this molten rock move so
slowly? new math, show me your work. part
marks for being born in time. is every fear
just a wish in a mask? and maybe matter's
only slo-mo packets of jellied pain, like how
ice is just slow water and steam is water in
a hurry. half the time i sit here like a piano
with a flat tire and beauty does all the heavy
lifting for me. there's a robot dog guarding
the neuron guarding the lo-res memory of
the spelling bee that stung me in 1983. there's
manacles of fog in the soap bubble kingdom.
how long this vertigo upon waking, these
tongues of flame above my bald spot?
the words for what i wanted idled in the
collector lane—oops! should i try mime or
binary code? at least with smoke signals
you could read between the lines. take
all my patents for the cold fusion reactor,
just tell me someone else, somewhere,
has ever felt this way. what way? exactly.

Holy Man Mistaken for a Scarecrow

factory speakers croon 'jesus take the wheel' but
it's not jesus leading me down a blind alley, it's
green lantern, it's renfield, dracula's loyal stooge,
it's my first kiss and the wizard saying pay no
attention to the man behind the curtain. later, i
grab hold of the forsythia, ride right through the
hurricane's eye. when the storm passes, the
sewer drains are plugged with broken toys. i
took the wrong things seriously, climbed the
wrong ladder, banged my head against the
cathedral gate as a d.i.y. penance. next time
use the doorbell, the sisters of mercy said, and
the door isn't even locked. cool that there's at
least one sanctuary of grace the mayor forgot
to flatten. sun-bleached roller derby advert
pasted over stained glass, boy bent double
by the weight of his textbooks, converting
fractions to ratios in his head. a blast of sun
churns his blood: you're only young once.
the holy man i mistook for a scarecrow
reminds me of a bridge i just can't cross,
burnt beans in the pan, the sapphire-studded
sci-fi backdrop that was really just a painting.

Lightning's the Difference

the bride lurches toward the patchwork monster
but she's only atoms just like the rest of us. daily
wedding of misaligned dust motes: no wonder
the scientist and the bridesmaids are draped in
black. so i eat that second helping of star seed,
alarm the health care professionals: lightning
grows from the ground up and so do i. lighting's
the difference between bride and scarecrow.
lightning's the world's pulse ringing in the ribs.
without it, no despair, no art, no painting of a
sky we mistook for sky. sorry captain america,
wrong number, and you never loved me anyhow,
always propping up dictators in banana republics,
playing security guard for the price gougers. on
the barton 2 bus the power and the glory
overtakes us, leaves us momentarily rattled,
weightless, but this pepsi still tastes like a
fire hydrant and the past is where i'm
calling you from. once i swallowed a bee,
once i sent an email i couldn't take back.
a cowboy walks into a bar. i mean, me. i mean,
a wall. dorothee tells me to grow a spine so i
plant a seed, watch it grow, wait for the
blooms that will turn all our scars into doors.

There's a Trick with a Guillotine I've Been Working On

that bouncer had no sense of humor. he should
have let me in for free, since i'm made of atoms
and atoms are mainly nothing at all. between
those atoms, just more nothing. that's why, if i
hold my breath, the executioner's blade should
pass right through me. in theory. wish me luck.
doordash messed up my order, gave me
trivial when i asked for eternal. i twist the
head off a boba fett doll in wordless fury,
frantically scan the headlines looking for
laughter amid the slaughter—two words
that should rhyme but, in fact, do not—a
poem amid the pillage, a slow cruel cull we
can dance to. disasters i can handle, it's the
dreary pinpricks of the day-to-day that grind
me down. how many liters in a dollar, how
many 9-11's in a pearl harbor. still i believe
in patterns, patterns buried underground
and patterns visible only from the air while
riding a pterodactyl made of stone. and all
because dorothee felt like taking a chance,
and the bus was faster than the train, and
there was a red balloon floating in a puddle
and she pointed and said hey look at that.

The Good Kind of Fire

run the numbers again: they have to add up to more
than that. raw datum of a discarded dime, stuttering
blip on the radar screen. your spirit animal's an
artificial fern. a thousand generations adored the
same moon you do, wept over the same birdsong.
friction burned away most of the meteor and the
express lane wasn't any faster: the customer
wanted a different sort of pear for a different
price; the customer wanted clarity; the customer
had a flier with a price-matching guarantee.
the manager carried the one, realized the extra
three bucks an hour wasn't worth it. adjust the
frequency and everything's burning; adjust it
again and it's the good kind of fire, the kind that
refines, that sunders pure gold from duplicitous
alloy. now i'm back in the waiting room, staring
at a poster of the human glandular system—all
her strange and intricate highways—and feeling
sorry for the mute extras in crowd scenes in old
action movies: people shouldn't feel like they're
extra because nobody is. we're all essential:
the milky way wouldn't be the same without us,
even if only the roses recognize me, while the
hero gets a gold medal for saving the princess.

Internal Combustion Moratorium Resolution

rancid creosote fumes leaking from discarded railroad
ties, denuded scrapyards, defunct refineries, the
desperate housewives of atlanta leering at me from
the magazine racks: the sun stands still as visa
ponders whether to approve my transaction—with
existential dread like this, who needs hollywood?
how truly swaddled in flame this life is! steam engines
took us too far, internal combustion even farther.
images are blurry this far from the launch pad.
slippery as an atom's ghost, a tap-dancing hint of hope
challenges the daily doom with a plastic batarang
but doesn't replace it, not quite. in the food court
there's a deal on burrito supremes. the regulars barter
their scrips for lorazepam, xanax, various other benzos,
with tall tales of iou's from back in the day. the
dinos dream of revenge upon their replacements.
faith tiptoes like a burglar and needn't bother;
we forget so easily, leave flaked-off shards of soul
in the blue recycling bin. once i read a book. the
author died a week after he wrote it, yet his final
words sang of the future, and universal salvation.
i sneak up on strawberries in case all those
seeds are eyes. i take a yellow highlighter to
random bible verses, looking for loopholes.

Day of Reckoning in a Recycled Reality

still can't believe they paved over red hill creek.
every year on that fatal anniversary i sleep under
the overpass and read a book about trees. every year
a different page jumps out at me. wish hard enough
and the shade of the honey locust can rock to sleep
the cosmos we knitted out of doll parts and tinfoil.
stephen hawking says every star hides a scar.
what's it like to be a constellation? holding the
same pose for a billion years can't be good for
the circulation. a day so oily it can't be caught:
the panhandler thinks out loud, balances on one
foot, stretches out his arms (high above him a
hawk describes a lazy spiral) and suddenly it's
hard to care about interest rates, stagflation,
the word i misheard by the victory fountain.
lonely neural net like a monster under the
bed in a dream you can't wake up from.
hipster so rude to the waitress it's enough
to make you wish there was a hell. eviction
notice on the wind turns to wind in the end.
just because it's called a fault line doesn't
mean the fault is mine, the earthquake explains
to the disaster area. after all that screaming,
turns out the scariest part is the echo.

Rocket Surgery, not Brain Science

threw on the wrong head today: this face really
doesn't match these pants—a fatal fashion
faux pas! asked a crow for flying lessons, the
crow said it really comes down to a positive
mental attitude, which means there's a lot of
walking in my future. it all finally made sense,
why the universe is relentlessly expanding,
when an ex called collect from cape breton
nova scotia to say she needed more space.
i don't know me, not even my favorite color.
who said magenta? what happened to blue,
and charles foster kane's childhood sled? the
musical chairs reboot is casting for extras, but
there's a new deadly urgency this time around.
mistress nemesis is taking no prisoners.
can i at least choose the song? oh, the fine
print already covered that? carry on then.
chains of smoke hold me fast, and there's a
hint of a calm beyond all knowing, and
why doesn't grace knock a little louder? by
the time i finished changing the sheets,
the tree out front had grown another ring!
what if the magic never really left us, and
my true self is a genie in a bottle, freed.

Too Much Darkness for the Night to Hold

maybe i shouldn't have bet it all on a dead horse.
there's always an explosion breathing down your
neck, and even the flora and fauna are stuffed
with prophecy. lost among the weeds, a plot
twist that would have redeemed everything.
good and bad ride on the same coaxial cable so
you may find yourself doing what you don't want
to do, desiring more when you know you're full.
that's a lot of cold starts for one wrinkly brain. *when
the transmission goes, i go,* were its famous
last words. so many trips to the scrapyard
replacing spare parts, i don't feel like me anymore.
stainless steel hubcap where a knee used to be.
weird bonfire fueled by smiley-faced report cards.
we're the undefeated, the unhoused, the kids
who bring cotton candy cones to a gunfight.
found a larva in my hypo; didn't even complain.
i always grab the wrong word from the knife
drawer but silence is even riskier so mime isn't
for me, neither is hide-and-seek, and the free
market said no thanks to a double agent who
can't keep a secret. think of a phone booth in
a food court in a dead mall wired for
detonation. that's where i'm calling from.

Acorn at the Bus Stop

when they ask me for a reason, i tell them about the
swarms of dots ever swirling before my eyes, and
riots of daisies gumming up the efficiency reports.
how rarely the smile fits the skull, or punishment
the crime. hard labor for a momentary bout of
blasphemy while the trillionaire gets a slap on
the wrist for dooming an unborn generation.
in the time it took to slap, compound interest
reduced us all to tools anyway. we're all doing
a dine-and-dash from someone else's point of
view, and some checks you can't dodge forever.
for the crucifixion scene, rembrandt gave the
disciples the faces of his next-door neighbors
and he *still* couldn't stay ahead of the repo man.
some souls are black holes and vice versa but
that doesn't make this moment exist any less
enthusiastically. sunrise obliterates my master
plan like an elephant stomping a scrabble board.
there's an acorn at the bus stop hoping for some
luck, tolstoy dying at the train station and a
river that meanders but is never truly lost.
there's no mountain that won't one day melt like
a sugar cube in the rain. will this be on the final?
when you're a big boy, every day is test day.

Heroic Return Seen Through Broken Glass

plastic adventure man fights his way out of his
comic book's pages and onto the balcony. the
night reeks of cut grass and buckets of regret.
he doesn't need his radioactive magic to know
something's wrong. he remembers holding the
golden scream of power in his hands, solving
the riddle of quantum entanglement, catching
every green light all the way home. flatland's
fairy-tale logic made him grow overconfident;
he forgets the magic word, his x-ray vision
runs away on him, now when he looks up the
sky's an iron dome, the horizon line an angry
fractal. blinded by memories of a mirror
kingdom, an apple tree that couldn't believe
in winter, he knows his voyage ends not with
a homecoming but with signing the doctor's
dreadful paperwork. why must our true home
always be in another world? the hero lets it all
go: the lust of result, the wicked finish line mirage.
but hero is a funny word when there are
galaxies of mystery in every broken window.
so many things i can't explain to her. so many
elephants dancing on the same tightrope.
even the shadows are shaped like spies.

Does the Ash Remember the Fire

a black hole eats a world, asks what's for dinner.
made the same mistake so many times the
simulation gave me frequent flier miles.
a rowboat enters the tunnel of love, exits
as a fire-breathing dragon. my doctor
says my bloodwork makes him sad.
quantum fields between rivers of dust,
devilish illusions of skin, dreams of
the real slippery as ice. it's all been
downhill since opposable thumbs. past
and future circle each other like gladiators,
like resentful exes still hot for each other.
know thyself? if i knew myself, i'd run away.
does the ash remember the fire, the flat
champagne the bubbles? i always studied
the final credits, hoping i'd see the names of
old roommates, then remember it's a silent
movie from 100 years ago and nothing lasts,
even boulders are just clouds with different
frames of reference and a lot more patience.
closeup of the tramp, his eyes, his lover.
wide shot of the two of them, bravely
marching into the unknown future.
curtains. applause. more curtains.

Golden Tinsel

attn: every blade of grass, every grain of sand, i'd
feel bad if even one of you were destroyed in a
transporter beam malfunction, or crushed under
the weight of a long-dead soviet satellite that swung
too low and couldn't resist earth's fatal attraction.
punched holes in the walls, can't remember why.
when dorothee came home, i blamed it on mice.
she didn't buy it; i doubled down, laid out two kinds
of mouse traps, old-fashioned and modern, then
declared victory when no more holes appeared. if
only you could channel your genius into something
positive, superman told lex luthor, but ask a brick
to grow wings, a vortex to stop eating, or a
rocky mountain to quit poking holes in the sky.
then tell city hall to stop bulldozing the past to
make room for a monorail nobody voted for.
the hard part of magic's the coming down and
remembering you still have to keep your tax
receipts, no matter how many rabbits in how
many hats. outside's a dove: such a mighty
howl for such a tiny throat, a protest against
the world of forms and the shadows they cast.
a swan weaves golden tinsel into her nest,
leaving me so shocked i don't blink for months.

Between Two Magnets

found a suitcase full of nooses in the basement,
can't imagine how it got there. magic used to
grow on trees: now it's all about the 0's and 1's.
we dress for success, chase a shiny red ball, until
the undertaker gives the referee the fatal, final signal.
the styrofoam resurrection's for subscribers only.
surely a few of those footprints in the snow are mine.
ditto those sweaty hearts carved in the frosted glass.
but you know this already. but you aren't even here.
the rocket ship is out of gas, the beach is out of sand.
try apples from a different farmer: nothing changes.
sculpt origami monsters from loser lottery tickets.
count drone strikes while held hostage by a red light.
darth obnoxious, meet darth prepaid automatic billing.
there's a magnet under the mud, turning my flip-flops
into massive frankenstein clogs, and it's true: life's
the dream of weightlessness between two magnets.
there's a prehistoric blueprint guiding our zombified
commute, and ghosts yelling out play-by-play from
the sidelines. behind my scar's a ticking time bomb
and a wind-up mini-gorilla, raging against his cage.
i stand on ceremony, salute every tree and pothole.
never thought the joke would get so far out of hand.
never should have let the monkey take the wheel.

Labyrinth Diary

another day, another stutter in the simulation.
the mind and the brain start growing in different
directions, sleeping in different beds. i used to
run to the mirror in the middle of the night just
to make sure my reflection was still there. the
boss showed his appreciation with moldy cake
and hawaiian shirt day. it's a bit much when the
monkey runs away with the instruction manual.
the amazon driver leaves the lipitor in the wrong
mailbox, takes a picture, walks away. a honeybee
headbutts the frosted glass, finally surrenders,
curls up on the granite countertop, homesick
thorax twitching in distress, a stale-dated sos.
the inbox chokes on legends of multiple income
streams while i double down on the insect
kingdom–they know something we don't.
some days in the maze i give my cerebrum
a vacation, just hulk-smash right through
the thorny brambles and let the blood flow.
greedy lava gobbles up garden gnomes and
ornamental shrubbery. new stories rise out
of the destruction. some of them are true. at
least the lemon tea is real, and waking up and
not knowing if i'm upside down, or the world is.

Bless the Bricks

a man lost in a blizzard sticks out his thumb.
drifting snow masks his distinguishing marks.
he could be anyone, a nobody or a hero. a
man in the carlton tavern tells me the earth
is flat. there's mustard in his beard, peanut
shells on the floor. we both can't believe
how late it is–that calendar can't be right.
but i think of goya, and lou, all the greats
who died just like i will, and spending all
night on the fire escape behind the tivoli
theater and now there's divinity enough
for us all, with bushel baskets left over.
how many parking meters for how many
paper plates at the knights of columbus
charity barbecue; how many obsolete
computer languages for how many
sisters of mercy, blessing the bricks
of the comatose westinghouse plant?
the rage of the downsized of ward 3
is set to a perpetual simmer. without
dorothee i could survive it all not at all:
think of the calculus that keeps the moon
from crashing into the sea, or a high-wire
elephant hanging onto a ladder woven
from spiderwebs. that's what it feels like.

Bloody X on the Treasure Map

and there were years when nothing happened.
neighbors greyed incrementally. blank spots
in my work history just dared me to say
something. i counted syllables in the high-
tension silence, subdivided samosas into
wafer-thin slices, asked the angels for a
recount. other years it was everything all
at once: sunrises knocked the wind out of
me; ditto politicians, with their baffling
musical chairs routine. i'm like the chatty
fifth wheel at the séance, laughing at the
wrong time and bursting the occult bubble
just before grandpa's ghost reveals where
he hid the family fortune. a squirrel stares
at me like it knows all my secrets until i start
blushing. imagination's playful even in its
terrors, remember that double-parked
monster truck crushed by mothra, the
canned laughs on the parents' landline.
tibor tells tales of public hangings and
firing squads, savagely honks his horn
at a shell-shocked racoon. our shared fury
builds a sort of bridge. i count up my
microaggressions like a miser with his coins.

Spoon on a Chair

my brain's not like a computer at all, i wish
they'd stop saying that. i practice jumping
because the farther i am from the earth's
core the greater the odds of kissing a bird
or hugging a comet. one time a dog-faced
cloud followed me home, but my landlord
said no pets. the next morning revealed a
regret-shaped puddle by the welcome mat.
a spoon reclines on a chair and i'm staggered
by all the mining and grinding and commerce
that got it there, the quicksand physics of it all.
a plate falls from my hand, explodes like a
bomb, what a shock. my hands are steady.
real bombs are falling far away. sloth, self,
sleep, screens—my laptop doesn't taste like
salted ham even though my inbox is full of
spam, no i don't want to insure my life, or
meet someone new. i want a bigger window
when divebombing starling murmurations
strobe shadows across the meadow. but
i'm a stranger to myself, like that astronaut
who returned home with expired passwords.
something happened to him up there. this
new director's cut is full of rotten easter eggs.

In Heaven

nameless moth headbutting 7-11's neon signage,
if only this gorilla could kiss you without crushing
you. martin called for a revolution but if the world
revolved any faster i'd get so dizzy i couldn't
remember my name. there's a whale at seaworld
that outweighs this bus, and morlock drones who
never caught a break—the market's algorithms
grew cold, then cruel. humans trip right over angel
ephemera on their way to dollar tree. the lonely
match in iron man's heart flickers ominously:
one strong breeze and it's curtains for the hero.
the next time we argue over bath towels, remind me
to grow wings first. i'll rise, hover, rise some more,
hide behind the moon until the dark rage passes.
a kid got stabbed over a pikachu pokemon card,
gravity's a joke we tell ourselves while waiting
for the kettle to boil, and the western hemisphere
really doubled down on right angles and compound
interest! while the billionaires forgive each other for
everything, i want to fly as close as i can to the sun
without burning my umbrella. in heaven, will i still
miss my 10-speed raleigh bike, the one the local
bully stole just to teach me a lesson about what
really fuels the world's engine? trust me: i learned

That's How I Remember It

that whole year i dreamed about the ocean.
tv preachers were my guilty pleasure. there
were pre-paid long-distance miracles and
lonely widows looking for a sign. newsmen
prayed for war, a chance to really shine.
the future was for verified subscribers only.
potus dangled the nuclear option to draw
attention away from his hair plugs. there were
days when time stopped, days where i was
overcome by an urge to be in two places at
once, like when you want to sleep in but also
want to explode into 1000 legendary pieces.
even the hotties were simultaneously dancing
and disintegrating—a ghoulish juggling act.
camaros on blocks were particularly poignant,
so were racoons frozen in the strobing glare,
and the way i bonded with strangers as we
marched in line in the parade of wounds.
my pockets were stuffed with palindromes.
often during late night safaris i'd find i already
had what i was hunting for. people asked me
if i was being sarcastic but i swear i never was.

Rivers of Gold

when the daylight gives me the shakes i call my
recovery buddy, she's addicted to birdwatching
now, says, you know the dates are all wrong,
the pyramids are a lot older than you think,
and my battery is about to die, so talk fast. i
know she's lying. about the battery, not egypt.
at least there'd be static, something to cling to,
if we still used landlines. all the sounds of the
natural world are muffled by air brakes and
ronnie screaming at olivia about pulling her fair
share. off in the margins: swans, carburetors,
crackpots, castaways and the passing parade.
there used to be a word for this but every new
year the dictionary gets thinner and thinner.
a hummer cuts me off in the bike lane, i follow
it for a mile, plotting chokeholds and quick shots
to the kidneys before the rage melts into a dull
fog. i start looking for landmarks, the north star
or the golden arches. the evangelist in the dog
park, his clothes are so tattered i stick around
for the whole boring sermon. when leaves curl,
knowing their time is up, there was a word for
that too. if it was up to me there'd be rivers of
gold everywhere. tomorrow i will kiss a rose.

Playing Hopscotch with a Cloud

wrap the house in tinfoil and your batteries will last
longer. when earth is closest to mercury,
advertisements are harder to ignore; it's like
uncle sam is pointing right at you. mr. kool aid
man said what good's a missile silo without
any missiles, and without sugar where would
all those dentists be? nowhere, that's where,
and roaming the parking lots for cars with keys
left in the ignition. tony the tiger called me a
sheeple, asked me why i was so blind. told
him the farther we got from the big bang the
more i need a flashlight, even the bottom
shelf of the fridge is a lost continent. smug's
not a good look, tony, st. francis was right,
even if half his twitter followers are bots. this
finch is real, its ancient call, the way its wing
slices the air into parcels of quanta. never
seen her panic, she trusts her instincts.
some days even the rubies taste like oreos.
bumped into a cloud i'd played hopscotch
with back in kindergarten—small world.
what would mini-me say to me? if i'd known
about the cubicles waiting up ahead for
us, i'd never have stopped hopping.

Scar of Unknown Origin

the idea behind all that frantic scribbling, all those
cartwheels, was to keep the poison tide away
from my heart, to slow down the rate of decay
and buy another spin of miss fortune's terrible
wheel. the idea was to think like a rock, to run
like water. i like to wake up before the world
does—nothing's more accurate than silence—
before the dark and the dawn, the chimneys
and the hawks, start their ancient duets.
the sun burns, howling air brakes give my
soul's own pulse an industrial staccato beat.
i suck in my gut, dye my beard, fool no one.
the mk-ultra grad preaches to the trees in
gage park before scouring the earth for
scrap bits of copper wire. there's something
precious in the pockets of the runner who
endures to the end, it adds up to something,
not nothing, and we deserve more parades,
says the steelworker who was replaced by
a robot arm. in my heart i know he's right,
suddenly it's years later, i've got a new scar
of unknown origin and new dead ends on
the gps. i've been this way for awhile now.

Politics of Comets

thanks for asking. the shawarma hut is right where
you left it. some of the slogans on the billboards are
different. a monkey told me we're distant cousins
today, asked me for a loan. what could i say? i'm
already paying off one credit card with another.
the staples in my neck remind me i'm turning into
dad, how's that for a twist? we never could agree,
on creases in dress pants or the hottest ticket to
heaven. up there, you never have to apologize,
or wonder about your true place in the milky way
galaxy. stelco's nefarious oxides fog my glasses.
dusk, bedazzled in sequins, needs me not at all.
tremors, born deep underground, remind me of
dreams lost at sea, kindly granduncle faces at
bygone family reunions. I see broken windows,
and doors nailed shut. a woman with only one
shoe howls for justice. just for kicks i tell the
missionary, no, i'm not born again, look: i only
have one bellybutton. the baffling byzantine
politics of comets and lost mittens back me
into a corner. i howl, puff out my chest like
king kong. nobody ever asked me, they just
went ahead and rezoned everything, and the
dress rehearsal turned out to be the real deal.

That's Not a Zipper, That's a Scar

groaning earthworm stranded on a concrete island,
when i picked it up and dropped it into the garden
dorothee called me a hero. consolation prizes
lurk like spies in the strangest places, like that
barn swallow feathering her nest with tinsel,
and ropy pre-dawn helical bands of mist make
me forget about scammers dodging subpoenas,
robber barons declaring bankruptcy and leaving
no forwarding address. too much caffeine and
I slip into a parallel world organized around a
different vibratory principle. wildflowers grow
wilder there. cherubs are more than just rumor.
and no sequoia is ever culled and pulped for
junk mail. over here, the grand geometer's
been cutting corners again—just look at the
faces of the lovers in the hallmark christmas
movie, all their tears look painted on, even
their exit wounds have continuity errors.
always hated it when movie rifles sounded
like pistols, it really broke the spell. my
lifeboat's on fire, my ringtone's a wolf. still
can't believe spielberg didn't answer
any of my letters. don't tell me to
calm down, I'm calm as a clam.

My Doombot is Late

all the newsboys had their war faces on
so turtle eggs under the trestle went
unreported, but it was still a miracle.
had the dream where running backward
is a secret key, flicked the lights on too
fast and caught the roaches stealing the
brie, blushed, grabbed the wrong remote
and a star died screaming, so far away
nasa won't notice until ad 10,000.
capital one says I should be debt-free by
then, hashtag winning, hashtag bastards.
dear re/max realty, flip this town as
often as you want, the natural world
will not be denied. here she comes now,
poking her snout through the chain
link fence at king william and ferguson.
the sign says luxury lofts, the sky's a
pepsi blue, stolen shopping carts are
stuffed with flyers. my doombot is late,
stuck in traffic or just toying with me
like a cartoon cat with a cartoon mouse.
everyone's someone's looney tunes ghoul,
waiting for the meteor and battling
dragons with wet firecrackers.

Valentine with Speed Limit

i might listen to an oracle if i ever met one;
so far it's just been fellow humans all the
way down. i think my first thought was a
wordless joy at the thrum of my mother's
pulse. my last thought was about mafia
hit men in 70's cop shows. how fast
thought travels! faster than the cartoon
tarpaulin they threw over summer, and
hey, give me back my beach ball. taxis
are slow on the inside, faster on
the outside when you're late and
spiraling toward the event horizon at the
milky way's heart. i wonder if rembrandt
knew when it was his final brush stroke.
i wish we could take this beach home
with us. today could have used a few
more stitches where the sea meets
the sand, but you're so beautiful—
even your toes!—that i stopped
keeping score a long time ago.

All I Know

all i know is what i have words for and that's
not much. you could win the lottery, rename
every street in hamilton and mirror, mirror,
nothing would change at all. we're always
building traps for ourselves to fall into,
beartraps lurk in our own dna spirals—
such microscopic duplicity, when even
the subatomic is suspect. the cool dude
in the record books for eating so many
hot dogs in so many minutes will soon
be replaced. every clock a traitor, every
witness an accomplice, the monitor
taped to the chest turns the heart's
frantic murmurings into long strands of
zeros. i'd like a second opinion: denied.
i'd like a fresh pen: denied. meaning of
life etched on mist; a song in bloom
we edited out of the cash grab reboot.
grandfather-wracked-in-pain-shaped
cloud. slow sexy camera pan over cgi
sadism; our souls meet at the bottom
of a bag of popcorn. history hovers,
holds its breath. things get so crazy,
even the smarties taste like diamonds.

Truth in Advertising

there's an overdose and a hunger strike at the
barton jail, and a fire alarm without a fire, but
that wasn't me, that was the me from 5 minutes
ago. you can't kiss fast enough to kiss the same
sidewalk twice, everything's changing that fast.
tranqs for the memories, martin would say.
and what good is an anchor carved out of
cheese, or a parachute made out of clay?
and why's beauty so barbed with briars, why
can't i go straight to the ice cream sandwich
without the middleman's whiptrack scars?
ever wonder if spam email is the moon's
revenge for all that litter the astronauts
left behind? questions like these keep me
awake for days. still feels like a win whenever
i wake up anywhere besides a stranger's
bathtub. remember the book whose author
died, coughing up blood, before finishing
the last chapter? that's what our first date
reminds me of: wet firecrackers for miles.
the next time i change careers i'll try being a
cro-magnon hunter/gatherer. farewell, velcro!
hello, goblin-haunted world devoid of clocks.
love claims more victims than lions but you'd
never know that from the travel brochures.

Blue-Collar Harlequin

smelling, in the dark, the rank reek of new-mown
lawns—choking on it now—i pretend bad luck isn't
a thing, remember that once there was a saint
who lived up in a tree for 38 years as if sin were
an airborne germ, and maybe he had a point.
fast-forward 15 centuries and an ex surprised me
when she married a private detective. by the 1st
anniversary the glamor was long gone, she sent
me a text saying, i think i made a mistake. i think
of swamps and glens in old paintings, my savage
ancestors glaring down at me disapprovingly as
i scrabble through a maze of peep shows and
shooting galleries. never thought i'd miss working
at the balloon factory, coming home spattered in
blobs of colored latex like a blue-collar harlequin.
my roommate said i should change my name to
abstract arthur, art for short, and i never thought
i'd miss kissing the moon in the gutter, or waking
up wearing someone else's name tag. funny how
some nights, when you say, thank god it was just a
dream, there's another dream waiting for you in
the knife drawer, the laundry hamper. voices
fly like bullets over still water, and it doesn't
even matter if the words are true or not.

Tent City in the Auto Graveyard

stripped oldsmobile perched on cement blocks,
mcmansion plantations tottering away from us on
rickety stilts, abraded bits of gray matter tap the
mat, the coach throws in the towel but the
damage is done. in the slums of my cerebral
cortex there's a drowned eden and a cowboy
lost in the wrong movie. ping-ponging off my
skull is an infinite echo of armies of zeroes.
behind the denim, a tattoo. behind the tattoo,
a wind-up mini-gorilla chipping away at my ribs.
pockets laden with loyalty rewards cards,
the way she moved on after the mutiny
without a single souvenir, the farewell
scene at the train station botched by a
rookie editor. jump cuts like strobe lights.
non-union stagehands patch the holes
in the sky of our cage. un-friended and
re-friended so many times i stopped getting
my hopes up. i knew a guy who, when he
played russian roulette in the southern
hemisphere, slapped the chamber up
instead of down, just to be polite. my
hallucinations are full of plot holes.
my first car was a 98 oldsmobile.

Rainbow Reflected in a Bubble

we dress for success and a shiny red ball
until the cardiologist tells the referee to
blow the whistle. and for this the king sold his
kingdom! granted, it was mainly swampland.
we hunker down, ignore the s & p 500, boil
lentils, recite psalms. the snow falls, drifts,
a blast of truth like a neon smudge rocks
the entire kitchen, i swear this is the truth.
the welder next door screams at his wife
so the whole block can hear, something
about money, and how many more times.
hovering above us, another us entirely,
untainted by the pollution of childhood,
like the idea of a rainbow reflected in a
bubble. stubborn scent of spiderwebs
and lead in the pipes. does this milk
taste funny to you? every sip reminds
me of the rotary phones we discarded
just because the future told us to. now,
necromantic chants are my ringtone.
warm light bending around the curve of
this apple, a glint of glitter in the cornea,
should be all the divinity we need, and
music is nice but silence is even better.

Memory of Mercury

cheer up, she said, someday you'll be a skull,
and skulls are always smiling, so start practicing
now! i said, i think it's time for me to find a new
therapist. even before the transplant, i had
always suspected my brain was second-hand.
like a hitchhiker in a snowstorm i try to talk
myself in off the ledge: after world war 3
we'll look back on this and laugh, etc. etc.
memory of a bartender building a tower out
of pretzels while explaining the antichrist's
master plan—i just wanted to talk about my
broken tooth, the rattling furnace i couldn't
afford to fix. tin man at the blood donor clinic,
mormon elder so nervous i almost convert
just out of sympathy. never thought i'd get
sentimental over a stripped mercury topaz.
guess you had to be there. can't believe i
shook a politician's *hand!* the ick of it all
haunts my hemispheres like a wicked
hocus pocus. never stopped feeling guilty
about that frog on the dissection table.
when the sun bleaches the color out
my grandma's old photographs, even
outer space will need a new coat of paint.

The Dragon and the Samurai

when you desire, that means something's
broken inside, microscopically speaking.
once dna spirals get tangled by vandals,
decades can fly by like wishing well soap
bubbles. but there's a secret me i keep
hidden, a hero's ghost invisible to eeg's,
ecg's and health care professionals. in
1815 beethoven said suffering is the only
road to joy, right before he said he could
hear the song of every tree in the forest–
a lovely thought. i know goya suffered,
and mom did too. there was something
i forgot to tell her, now i carry it, like a
planet stapled to my shoulder blades.
that's why i avoid stairs, rank dead last
in the annual around-the-bay marathon.
i painted a mural on the southern wall of the
royal bank the night before the demolition
crews arrived. the wrecking ball was the
point. i painted a dragon and a samurai.
below my signature i wrote *we're all just
particles, the dead only a little more so.*
there were happy endings, just out of
reach, and hidden cameras everywhere.

Story Sculpted from Dust

when you're zeus every solution looks like a
thunderbolt. but you can't go around incinerating
starter homes every time someone steals your
amazon shipment. loss is a subjective property.
the burn victim curses the triage nurse, not zeus.
the nurse has a restlessness she can't ignore, the
mindfulness workshop just left her feeling empty.
thought she'd *wanted* empty, but not *that* empty.
every atom everywhere swims away from each
other. the swimmer loses sight of the shore, and
dad spends more time on the road. rusty chains
clink in the fog. can't stop pinching you to make
sure you aren't dreaming. even a million isn't
what it used to be, and i thought you said we'd
only ever have to die once. ifrah's bracelet
screams from the sock drawer. i scan the rope
of my dna looking for the recipe for wings, for
courage, come up empty. that's a lot of wrong
numbers for one dismal nucleotide parade.
story without a hero, river sculpted from dust.
all of which is to say, here i stand, wishing i'd
brought some duct tape, preparing to battle
the secret landmine in my heart. these are
facts, but i never said i had an explanation.

Odyssey

back when i wrote crossword puzzles for a living
i solved mysteries on the side. the detectives got
jealous but couldn't argue with results. you'd be
surprised how often the butler really *did* do it. if
you had a butler. which i didn't. i didn't have
a lot of things. missing wives, missing cats,
broken homes, lone wolf psycho killers—
somebody killed miss america by turning her
into flowers. no clues. no motive. no leads.
only sweet-smelling lilac blossoms and some
embarrassed cops. when the trail went cold
they tried pretending it had all been a dream.
then they tried pretending *they* were a dream.
after that i quit, threw it all away. the skyline
was much too jagged, there was something
funny in the water. i ran all the way to arusha,
climbed mount meru. the sun drenched the
sky with flame. a monkey stole my lunch.
devoid of plans i gripped the earth with both
hands. i dreamed in black and white; heaven
laughed in technicolor. every cloud looked like
a celebrity. every wall grew wings. a 767's
vapor trail scarred the sky like punk graffiti,
that's when i knew it was time to go home.

Sun-Bleached Diary Entry from 1999

imagine days before the invention of calendars,
or a ufo that ran out of gas when it was only
halfway here. if humpback whales had been
the ones to wind up with thumbs, would they
have sprinted to extinction as fast as we do?
our scalps tingled, we ground our teeth down
to powder, she spoke of visiting her dad but it
never happened, there was the mystery of the
empty wallet, and the superstring spirograph
of shame. everything was so loud, even the
sunset as it threw a chill over huge parcels of
commerce and wildly optimistic renovations.
we got scared, ran all the way to taco bell but
eating just makes me hungrier, she said, *and
some souls are life jackets and some are
anchors.* always felt honored to be privy to
her private logic keys, her way of seeing
invisible connections. how i loved those days:
fighting the world with an empty notebook
and waiting for a miracle. my mind was open,
something somewhere was whistling.
imagine all our pregnant wins and losses,
swallowed up by an infinity of infinities. we
were royalty, and our castle went on forever.

Lost in the Future

still so angry, like when santa gave your brother
the toy you'd asked for, and then he never even
played with it. in sunday school they told you
cain was the *bad* guy, took away your gold star
when you wondered if he was just a victim of
bad press. put the mask on backwards and
the bus turned into a dragon, the future into
a declined debit card in the express checkout
line, how degrading. no one told the congress
of maples about the coming hyperinflation,
their shade blessing the beasts like a rumour
of another world, a royal decree from an
absent king. there was mold in the drywall
but a cheap roti hut next door so it all
balanced out. every day a *memento mori,*
a series of cracked-out calculations, grim-
humoured trade-offs. rate my bruise, kevin
said, does this look infected, do you have
any connections? we're apes in tracksuits
lost in the future and trying to memorize
the new rules. a siren reminds you of a
playground crush but it's hard to hear
much of anything when the roof's long gone.
shout into the wind, the wind shouts back.

Tornado Climbing a Ladder

the ministry of how may we help you teaches us
to lower our expectations, just like mom used to
do when santa was laid off right before christmas.
one by one the hypothetical lighthouses go dark.
a rolling blackout interrupts the miracle.
that new galaxy sure is pretty but maybe
it's just got a really good instagram filter.
unto us is given a finite number of disguises
so choose wisely and be polite: you never
know who you're really talking to. imagine
having angels stop by and serving them
leftovers, you'd never hear the end of it.
behind us a vast mountain is sliced away,
in front of us lies a daisy chain of movie
sets so hastily-erected the paint's still wet.
quirks and quarks like souls on parole
flood my retinas, make me see stars,
so no operating of heavy machinery
for a while. thanks for understanding.
go touch grass, wait for the great and
final untangling. if you need me i'll be
at my usual table, the one with the
chainsaw on the napkin and the crash
test dummy keeping me company.

Raining Frogs

thrush eggs were tanning in the midday sun
like haughty caesars. scattered pieces of a
low-flying heaven—timber, tinder, kindling,
cloud pillars—stomping the yard like
vengeful godzillas. we deserve no less: so
many ruined habitats and we never even
bought the dodo dinner first. how many of
my neural nets have been colonized by
2-for-1 specials and discount coupons,
and how many microbiomes perished
under my foot today? when it rained
frogs, that only hardened our hearts.
*'get a job, grind, something something
bootstraps,'* was a kind of magic spell
that kept us busy and blind. when love
rinsed my retinas a ghost was sitting
in my favourite chair. o simulated life
freckled with confetti! barbie and ken's
dream home will be radioactive for a
million years, and they gave us the
bulk rate at the crematorium as a
reward for our loyal patronage.

Kissing Azaleas

my right brain is unequally yoked with my left,
whenever it's not downright hostile. they can't
even agree on which way's up or down, never
mind how high's the sky, or how to save a soul.
the silence is oppressive until a kia sorrento's
burglar alarm starts howling. nobody moves.
most of the old gang has moved to the country.
i argue with a mad monk about pain being
wisdom's mother until pain shows up to break
the tie. the monk doesn't even say i told you so.
a toddler drops a lego, howls inconsolably like
it's the last lego in the world. disability liability
is unmade with one cruel keystroke: i see a
long chain of cardboard boxes, and nights
spent under the stars, looming in my future.
a cop tells me to stop kissing the azaleas, i
tell him to go catch some real criminals, and
just because you *can* turn your hand into a
fist, doesn't mean you *have* to. just because
the rust belt has conquered another county,
doesn't mean the story's over. somewhere
there's a rowboat, and a wall of mountain at
the end of the world, and a fairy tale that's
true. after all this, the cop smiles not at all!

Shaking Hands with the Big Dipper

the sun fuels the crops with a generosity that
leaves me starstruck, a newborn cloud molts
into a screaming skull but don't be shy, we're
all born screaming, so high-five, join the club.
perhaps all of matter is just a scream at room
temperature, and pain's the price of the blooms.
most of my life i just sat there: rusty landmine
in a fallow field; shifty summertime snowman.
gap-toothed piano bouncing on the diving
board, out of tune exo-ephemeralities. i'm
a betamax stack of grumbling fractions
and in this i'm not alone. chained to a flame
and waiting for dad in a room called *waiting,*
i choke on artificial light and purell hand
sanitizer. from geology's point of view, it's
all over except for the concession speech.
ask a rock: he'll tell you, walking upright is
just another ponzi scheme, a soap bubble
dream, gone too fast and here's the bill.
history's winners are just over there,
putting a fence around all the good stuff.
what if we still need something you can't put
a price tag on? don't ask the bargain hunters,
busily stabbing each other over free air miles.

Amoebozoa Orchestra

grabbed the sledgehammer instead of the
flyswatter—oops! someday we'll look back
and laugh. well, maybe not the fly. the
motivational speaker tells me i've wasted
my life: turns out all that birdwatching
didn't do much for the pension fund.
adulting is such a brutal zero-sum game.
it's even worse for aphids, ten days old
and they're middle-aged. yet i seem to
speak their language: clickety-clack of
alphas and alephs, whispered tales of
dreadful judgments and sugar-sweet
raptures. soon this aphid will die, bless
the soil as it disintegrates, every atom
a horny sacrament. there's music in the
dirt, and a lonely thought, a way of
anchoring oneself, almost got it–
until sirens, horns, and youtube shorts
do their patented smash and grab.
bucketful of hollowed-out nothing.
waterfall sculpted out of iou's.
winning ticket left unclaimed.
amnesiac superhero without a
song. tomorrow i will try again.

Half-Full Glass

recalled a rumor of a love that could walk through
walls, a coup attempt in the kingdom of the
blind. change is hard, algebra is harder,
ouch is the truth and forever is the sea. but
since when did the priest put jokes into the
liturgy? is theology just showbiz for ugly
people? was poetry easier a million years
ago? no past-due notices to kill your flow.
magnetic north was someplace else. so
much of the map was still up for grabs,
and blossoms were everywhere. what
if i'm only remembered as a shady
henchman in my archenemy's tell-all
memoir? what if summer never comes,
and the food factory runs out of tin cans?
no one's allowed forever but death is
always a surprise, someone else
always seems more deserving.
told the waitress to slap that baby
if he didn't stop whining; turned out
the baby was me the whole time!
still can't shatter a wall with my hand
but at least now it apologizes when it
gets in my way and i call that progress.

Crash Landing

you can count as high as i can but the first, last,
and fourteenth ways of looking at the buffalo skyline
are all mine—a few more truckloads of sod and
particle board and it might all add up to a point
of view. i mean, a lifeboat. i mean the emergency
exit in the x1 tie fighter leading the 61st squadron.
the golden ratio of meme to bloom, celebrity nft to
snapdragon's tooth, such a bounty of color leaking
from a single prism and today's not even a holiday.
and all the different kinds of sadness overflowing
inside my kaleidoscope: i earned my wings like
that crucified pterodactyl at the royal museum.
we both flew too high, had some awkward
moments on the way down. missed the
safety net. our cartwheeling silhouettes
left impact craters in the sidewalk like movie
star autographs. they flipped morning news
with evening news and no one even blinked.
mona lisa wouldn't smile like that if she could
see the 'kick me' sign they taped to her back.
never knew how lost we were until city hall
re-zoned our last orchard. i can't fix everything
but i can watch and wait, like the corner piece
of a polar-bear-in-a-snowstorm jigsaw puzzle.

Waiting for the A-Line, Dreaming of Monster Island

...and dreams chasing their own tails, woke
up feeling like a hasbro action figure
navigating a maze of deleted contacts.
the street was stuffed with umbrellas;
no sparrows anywhere. hard to find
the courage to impale the rain with a
trick arrow, harder still to imagine a day
that couldn't be improved by a godzilla/
mothra rematch. i could miss two stops,
have to run back to centennial, wouldn't
even care. somewhere between sunday
school and y2k gamera is still screaming,
sometimes my mind's a time machine
with a dead battery. throwing the spare
parts up in the air and making a wish
was always my default factory setting.
the future rubbed up against the disney
reboot, the friction bathing us in a flurry
of glitter. and everyone hated on the
princess, no matter how many charity
dinners she hosted it was never enough.
spent matches hissing in puddles, a
destiny you can't evade, my shadow
kickboxing against the night.

Naturopathic Remedy

today they will show us the frankenstein. it's our
reward for sitting through all those dull lectures
on amphibian mating rituals. the re-animator
ray dimmed the lights all over town. from inside
the oxygen tent, a hellish groan with a strange
accent. drunk dracula's down in the lab,
cooking up a fresh batch of larval-stage
tragedies and twist endings. king kong's
directing traffic at main and dundurn, the
homecoming parade got lost in the arctic,
amid rumours of yeti, and cannibalism—who
will dare to lead the sled dog rescue team?
we bet it all on less than a guess. click
here to prove you're not a robot. a tower-
of-babel-shaped cloud swallowed the sun. a
chipmunk with a limp lunged from the eaves
to a birch branch, its rib cage fluttering so hard
i felt responsible somehow, thought about
planting a tree, rescuing the princess until
all the crooked paths were hammered straight.
when it came to treating the crucifixion wounds,
watching the ballet of your fingers handling
the teaspoon worked better than anything
in all the medicine cabinets in the world

Skeleton Key Unlocking a Highway

looks like i confused the fast forward button
with the holy grail again, so sad. and the red
carpet they rolled out for us was the same
old river of blood. agnethe won't shut up
about her latest trip: what does it mean
when you see the dmt aliens and pierce
the veil of illusion and you still stiff the
waitress, tell the homeless to get a job?
the blindfolded knife-juggler would like a
few words with his guidance counselor.
so many blue ribbons in so many dead
computer languages. algol-68 might as
well be dinosaur-speak now. the college
filed for chapter 11 and meteors never
play fair. this wailing world, full of cracks
and fissures, papered over with bondo
and gorilla glue. dorothee's voice is a
skeleton key unlocking a highway.
her footprints radiate heat, and without
them i'd be lost in the woods, walking
forever in circles. such a cracked-out
odyssey from night to sight, and the
beauty of her movements—ever-new,
holy, and free of charge!—sends me.

Angry Ghosts of Bartonville

when the world's on fire is no time for waltzes
or watusis and yet here we are, slow dancing
our way out of the hostage situation gone
wrong. the tooth fairy with a dui, the iou
under the pillow. smooth jazz cover versions
of motley crüe flood the walmart; even the
sour cream curdles in protest. feral children
packed like circus clowns into shopping carts.
fluorescent tubes, their stutter faster than
hummingbird wings, throw off my rhythm,
leave me on the curb, knees above my head.
and all the bricks were styrofoam, that's how
we voided the warranty, clutching worthless
receipts, arguing with impassive umpires.
bartonville's founding ghosts don't approve
of what we've done to the place. somewhere
between light bulbs and velcro we should
have pumped the brakes. dead leaf clanging
against the electrified fence; headless malibu
barbie doll: souvenirs of a pilfered paradise.
weigh the body after death and there's always
a few crucial milligrams missing. so many
treasure maps we pulped into wallpaper. so
much gold dust we bartered away for tin.

Jenga Tower to Heaven Carved from Flame

my monster is almost ready to meet the lightning.
when the patchwork scarecrow animated by a
stolen fire runs amok, that might be a good time
to renegotiate my contract, ask for a parking spot
closer to the entrance. in the 1970's continents
were closer together, and ashtrays were
everywhere. parents loomed large, cast
giant chilly shadows. survived psychotic
presidents and botched amputations;
the little bits of you the lab sliced off
were cloned in petri dishes, released
into the wilds of the old growth forest.
the plane was on fire but i had a window
seat and the view of the sunset was primo.
jenneke said not caring was a superpower,
drive a nail through your head and still
she wouldn't cry, not since the age of
endless nights and shrieking dial-up
modems. our local representatives
can't agree on much, and that last
election didn't change a thing. a
murmur ripples through the 12-
items-or-less lane as the hungry
shoppers sharpen their knives.

Tongues of Water

even at midnight, earth from mars is bluer than
you'd think, and maybe i should have paid more
attention in sunday school. library patrons
complain i'm crying too loudly, a security guard
with delusions of rambo zip-ties me, stuffs my
mouth with rags, and shazam, i can't remember
my dreams, my name. picture a mind without a
head, smiley-face eyes without a smiley-face
mouth. details blur, wrinkles plow through the
1st, 2nd, and 3rd dermal layers. o to juggle
magnetic north and ground zero, to save the
lost lark, disoriented by rush hour traffic. time's
a heavy liquid and that's not a hot tub, that's
a swamp. zoom in or all the way out and
things are just as slippery: who knows
which late-night scam to bet on, or which
hyacinth branch is full of ancient magic?
how about that local sportsball team? we
made small talk, earned master's degrees
in dramatic disappearing acts. when the
collection agency caught up with me i ran
to the beach, woke up with sand in my mouth.
the tide's roar was like a lost language, and a
wave older than the dinosaurs held me tight.

Get Back in Line

the problem with the experts is there aren't any. where
were they when the sun blew a fuse, and capital one
mastercard stopped laughing at my jokes? experts
told us half-ton laser-guided raytheon bombs don't
hurt as bad when the good guys use them. and
you know who the bad guys are: they wear black
hats and threaten to lower your property values.
but weather laughs in the face of the weatherman:
promethean goldenrod bursting out of solid rock,
i hear you loud and clear. a thousand sin-soaked
pages and the bible never once mentioned search
engine optimization, there's a lesson in there
somewhere. get back in line, this illusion's all
mine. i'm some alien stranger's shooting star,
tragic case study in a textbook yet unwritten.
sith lord diorama at the walmart supercenter
performing gdp cpr, insolvency scapegoats
crucified on the golden arches. is a reverse
mortgage the right choice for you? asks the
demented 1970's tv detective. grief sliced
off bits of me until there wasn't much left,
and even big shots are just smiling piles
of glue and wire. so many stars shining down
and i've never even asked them their names!

Song for a Wicked Gorilla

won a prize, pulled down the pants of the debating
team captain, recycled the proles into spare parts,
still didn't learn a thing. snow tickled a founding
father cast in bronze, he meowed once, then
crumbled into dust. tried to evict a particularly
militant dust bunny via telekinesis alone:
results were unsatisfactory. here's a bomb,
straight from warner brothers. you have five
seconds. here's the frantically twirling
cheerleader you would have sunk the ships for,
and the girl whose heart you broke over a bad
connection. in 1946, city hall ripped all the trees
out of woodlands park just to punish striking
workers for seeking shade, true story. that's a
lot of sunburn to tell me what i already know:
there's no 3rd act karmic express mopping up our
spilled milk, and voting harder just makes it worse.
pick up the phone: the princess on the hill wants
to forgive you for everything. it's only her charity
that keeps you out of the wicked gorilla exhibit at
the metro zoo. elon's rocket ship left me behind
and i never even learned to tie a tie. this life's a
dream i had under grandma's hand-stitched quilts;
tomorrow's a toothpick sculpture built on sand.

Fistful of Dynamite

what's up with the wendy's drive-thru the morning
after a holiday, and what's up with stars, imagine
having so many arms. i meant to say, star*fish*,
and i meant to tell you something else at the
corktown tavern in 1999. my dream diary's caked
in blood. i mean ketchup. i mean my brain's not
a computer, it's a beehive, hear it humming from
lobe to lobe. being above ground's wearisome
but the alternative is worse. and what good's a
heart that's not been broken—that's like winning
a porsche and never bothering to crash it. the line
between treeline and sky is where the miracles
leak in, and usually stitched so tight not even
algae can squeeze through. that's why i never
leave home without a really big crowbar and a
fistful of dynamite. time's up! says the prophet,
but in woodland park's tent city there's nothing
but time, options narrow with every stopwatch
tick. pancake makeup sky smeared with fly ash
and powdered slag from dofasco's arc furnace,
cookie cutter cannon fodder, escape hatches
left untried, wedding rings lost in the weeds.
the sclerotic neon's a pentecostal vision and
no matter what i say, i mean something else.

The Heart of the Matter

life, ladies and gentlemen, is wasted on the living.
thought i was immune just because of a happy
face sticker on a report card in 1985. listened
to a veteran re-invent his past as the sun
beat down like a judge's gavel, fall asleep
in my steel-toes, woke up in someone else's
bathtub. the meaning of life wouldn't fit on
even a triple-xl t-shirt. a movie made me cry
on an airplane once, or was it the turbulence?
rolled my debts to the top of the hill in search
of wisdom. a russian monk held out his hand,
flame danced on his fingertips. asked if he
knew any shortcuts and he said not a word.
imagine rolling a boulder up a hill forever,
only it's not a boulder, it's fire, and it's not
a hill, it's time. the spaceman returned home
five hundred years late for dinner. so
many dirty socks on the stairs and i haven't
been cute since the age of vinyl and vhs.
if those terms are unfamiliar check the glossary,
ask a librarian, i'll be busy tunneling down to
the heart of the matter in a world of illusion
that's equal parts meat and magic, hunting for
the how of the what, and the how much longer.

Unicorn of the Year

today's a lot like yesterday—the same bungled
casseroles—but explain that to the trapdoor
spider, throwing silver threads across cruel
right angles, and to me, wired, not sleepy,
my anger melting into a puddle, the puddle
evaporating in the summer heat. something
crucial's been wired together with birdsong and
party streamers. senator chatbot has a glitch.
turns out some of our anime heroes were only
pretending, their robotech jetpacks just for show.
maybe it's not that bad, being a giant planet out
past the asteroid belt. or a snail, unless you forget
where you parked your shell. and a unicorn without
a horn isn't much of a unicorn, certainly not unicorn
of the year. maybe horses know the score: enjoy
what you have and stay out of fairy tales. my first
time seeing a real horse was a letdown, showbiz
had set the bar so high. o to be a leaf, all those
horny little veins singing the melody electric! ever
since eden the first frost is a little hard to believe.
it's natural to feel unnatural, and some days taste
like lint. swimming is fine but sinking is quicker.
we gamble on love while hiking the same
infinite loop. the path is made by walking.

Slowly I Unravel

all the emergency first responders are stuck in
quicksand. if there's a friend request, it's a bot.
pixel-patch sky above, play-doh ghost town below.
i trip on a tree root, split my lip, make a wish.
in dreams i kiss saturn's rings for good luck:
superstitious compensation for all the lonely
historical landmarks i sleepwalk right past.
at least the grackles and the jays, the dogwoods
and the cedars, are immune from such unhelpful
second-guessing. i hold my breath as the
honeysuckle winds itself around the trellis,
gives it a squeeze like a burmese python.
before paperless billing i dreamt the mailbox
was full of contraband kidneys and stem cells.
pretty sure the debt consolidation wasn't a
dream. by the time interest rates sliced my
heart right down the middle i was so numb
i didn't even ask for a band-aid. slowly i
unravel like a spiderweb on rewind, even the
wind blows my mind, knowing how many times
it's kissed you. you're my most mysterious
magic, i love watching you collect the
names of rose petals like secret keys.
it's funny: in 1989 i thought i knew it all.

Song of the Sleeping Security Guard

our screens boasted of higher resolution while we
grew vaguer and vaguer, couldn't even resolve that
last refund without threatening the nuclear option.
rolling blackouts interrupt the miracle. my head's
a match head waiting for a lucky strike. a book
on silent film stars wilts in the humidity, inky
marks run like cheap tattoos. we're all coasting
on the memory of ignition, the weightlessness
of smoke. can't remember which plague comes
next: a blizzard of dust or a river of styrofoam.
anything for a change in the weather. there's a
prehistoric blueprint guiding our zombie commute,
and ghosts calling play-by-play from the bleachers.
made a wish on the bridge but forgot to say presto.
the sacred river coiled itself around the padlocked
foundries and tin mills, then gave them a little hug.
the security guard neither observed nor reported.
to look at the sky is to look into the past but to
look into your eyes is to see a future stuffed
with wizards. there's something so romantic
about wave function collapse; i wasn't even
here at all until you noticed my potential. we
dole out descriptions, spit ions into the fire:
a quantum of time balanced on a seesaw.

Fragment from *The Encyclopedia of Worthless Superpowers*

it wasn't even a good party trick; lucas could ride
the go train, close his eyes, and see the final
destinations of all his fellow riders: long branch,
mimico, heaven, hell...it didn't get him on the
news, it just made him sad. i mean, sadder.
but his mutant power faded away when he
went gluten-free, now his guess is as good
as mine. think it all started with his mom's
mixed-up meds, a capricious flip of the
pharmacist's wrist. we're all static-age
children of the atom with radioactive tan
lines and they still can't fix the potholes.
someone cues up the laugh track from the
flintstones every time i stub my toe. i
sweat like the prince in that russian novel
who kissed the wrong girl in the dark.
california sinks into the sea just because
superman forgets to check his voicemail–
a new atlantis, a new reason to throw out
those dusty maps. all those state capitals
we learned just so we could lust over the
same parking spot. burn up the receipts
to ward off the frost. when the bill comes
due hold still: statues always ride for free.

Playing the Long Game

so here i stand, i can do no other, tracing the toronto
skyline with my thumb, inhaling/exhaling like an expert,
thoughtful as a twig, slapped silly by the market's
invisible hand, underqualified even to sit, to guard
traffic cones against an untrustworthy gravity.
helicoptering maple keys slam into the pavement
until i wish i'd brought ear plugs. tree rings play
the long game; tree rings know there's nothing
but time. becoming a stranger to myself–that's
not what the brochure promised me. did i really
buy acid-wash jeans without a gun to my head?
lost my cool over the wrong shampoo and now
a rainforest is gone, replaced by a gruesome
monoculture. miracles still bloom like litter
after the big game, but true atonement takes
years, a lifetime or longer. caught a train, felt
a murderous hatred for the brat kicking the back
of my seat until i realized he reminded me of me:
we both want what we want, and right now, not
later. and ice cream. and school's out forever.
sometimes the mummy trips over his own
bandages just before the showdown with the
archaeologist. sometimes there's a lily,
braving the frost and singing just for you.

Arboretum

each morning a hibiscus blossom; each night
a looney tunes mushroom cloud. days like
a choose-your-own adventure book with
random pages missing. stared at the tree
stump until the rings became a reflection,
an echo from a deep well. air brakes
squeal, roiling the aviary into a panic.
rainbow-spattered macaws slam into
the metal mesh fence and i think,
souls are like that, in their hair-trigger
jigsaw-style jitterations. some days i'd
rather not be a wrangler of unstable
molecules, mixing up the rate of their
half-life decay with the pulse of my own
lymph nodes. must be sweet to be a
billionaire's pet, a 3d nft. wait for the
chipmunk to eat out of my hand until
my arm starts to tingle but no dice,
he's been burned by primates before.
me too! tax the facts, print the legend.
there's fewer angels per square inch
ever since the rezoning, and i can't
even dodge the landlord without
leaving fingerprints everywhere.

Red Eye to Nowhere

...and windows without glass from simcoe to ferry
streets tell you a very strange story: a ghost story
without any ghosts. the wrecking ball's rezoning
permit taunts the sons of the pioneers. we used
to make studebakers, just over there; now all we
can do is play musical chairs, furiously bulldoze
the tent cities, overcharge for bottled water. we
should give the elephants a discount on peanuts
before we take the flamethrower to their last
cubic meter of habitat; just our little way of saying
oopsie. blinking brake lights at the mcdonald's
drive-thru tap out a secret code, and how many
times i've wished i could stick like glue, then i
wouldn't have lost so much mail to the dead
letter office. maybe if i'd said please. please
oceans, please six flags roller coaster, please
red eye to heaven, even if the pilot's hammered
and the play-by-play guy is talking backward.
can't even tie my shoes anymore without the
director's dvd commentary cheering me on.
all those x-ed out calendars, and calluses
on dad's twisted hands. lonely bee dancing
all alone. if i'd known it would take this long
i would have asked for a window seat.

Downtown's a Treacherous Imp Spinning Gold into Velcro

find a plum tree swaddled by an aphid swarm, take
it pretty hard, like that lego super-sculpture—
destroyed by one malicious big-brotherly kick—
i know i'll never forget. world war three fever
marches ever closer to the front page and noah
won't stop talking about his job welding ladders
onto rail cars. he gags on solder and spent wire.
tiny bits of airborne slag from the flex core's arc
follow him around like a guilty conscience and
overtime's triple-time on christmas eve. abigail
weeps over a dead scratch card. i tell her luck
like hers can't last forever but what do i know.
short-timers caked in grime line up, swipe out.
fashions change, leave us behind; some years
we don't even bother to change the calendar.
lonely pilot lost at sea, lost even to history. no
moon; just a balloon. even the fog smells of tar.

One Holy Clue

is this really part of the test? what happened
to privacy? but okay, the answer is e, all of
the above. i did all those things in the 20th
century, and it's all my fault. and yes to 17 c:
the squatters' hotel is right where you left it.
but the shawarma hut is a starbucks now, in
the chilly shadow of the health ministry towers.
bet if we dug up the time capsule we buried
by the monkey bars, we'd find it had sprouted
nyarlathotep-style tentacles and a freddy
krueger mask. an ill-timed stutter is enough
to make me a prime suspect–the cops in
this town are so *lazy!* if lieutenant columbo
was my friend i'd phone a friend for sure,
he could straighten all this out, find the holy
clue the tunnel-visioned lifers missed.
bumping rails at the midnight laundromat
yakking about old-time cowboys, thinking
about starting over as mountain men but we
couldn't start a fire with matches, let alone a
damp fistful of twigs. the trail of bottle caps
we dropped so we wouldn't get lost glinted in
the gloaming like the tarnished medals of
brave soldiers who never made it home.

Parking Lot Theophany

the day's ligaments shimmy out of focus, shriek
like an old-time radio stuck between stations.

without complaint, a sick pine absorbs the
expressway's diesel fumes. the family farm

waves the white flag as asphalt spreads
like cancer. a celebrity divorce turns ugly:

she changed her mind, she wants it all. a
pristine iron man doll guards the landfill

as we forage for leftovers in the near dark.
the wind rattles the flagpole; faster than

sentences it's miles away. look at
that, i say. look at what, she says.

a tightness in the chest, then a dizzy
elation like a great dream of heaven—

Motivational Seminar at Ground Zero

why should only the sane be allowed to make
all the big decisions? so far, their track record
hasn't exactly been stellar. just the other day
the sane poisoned an ancient aquifer and
called it job creation—a dirty trick the insane
would never think of trying; they're too busy
considering the lilies of the fields, wrestling
with shadowy calculations they don't have
words for. nestle and pepsi robbed us of
the old deep magic. try a hard reboot:
niagara falls is running low on memory.
the strobing harvest moon says check
engine light soon. even port dover beach
grows gleefully duplicitous—i wish the tide
could roll in and out just once without
reminding me that only i can prevent
forest fires. still, there's something regal
here that can't be denied, all the daffodils
and flagpoles bow low in solemn homage.
the melody lingers long after the lyrics.
never did finish that rubik's cube. on our
first date, the wind shook the trees,
christening our quest with perfumed
blossoms, that much i know is true.

If I Had a Car

clickbait frisbee tricks leave me hollowed-out
and convinced there is some fun somewhere
i am missing out on. naturally i respond by
dialing old phone numbers and updating my
linkedin profile. if i had a car i could wrap it
around a tree, or drive until the pain faded
and the third-act gambling debt was paid off.
but my license is just for show now, and to
prove i'm me, and cars are so antisocial:
if it wasn't for bus drivers I'd have no friends
at all. down by cootes paradise marsh, the
desjardins bridge groans under the weight
of trucks and even a power-mad parliament
can't hold back the spring: i cheered when
the weeds colonized the toxic brownfield. the
blazing spokes of the day spin like pinwheel
firecrackers. not long ago, slow wi-fi wouldn't
trigger a panic attack. and there was no i.d.
in pockets, and no pockets, just smiling
hunter-gatherers. we went from caveman
bikinis to iron man armour in the time it takes
to punch a hole in the sky, and why is rain?
because the sky is crying. why is the sky
crying? probably something i did years ago.

Dumpster Diving Void Warranty Blues

do these memes make me look fat to you? forty
open tabs and i can't even promise to try harder.
imagine prowling room to room with nothing but
the walls to kiss, and no gold coins to inherit–
so fast it barely happened at all, a sparrow looms
at the glass, divebombs, disappears and i'm
undone, miles from home, lost hero of a lost
battle. there are mansions on the hill, left-handed
wrenches and daffy ducks with beaks blasted
backward. i've got a squeaky boot, no money
for duct tape. friday crawls over mount albion
falls as gross profits piss all over history. it's
pathetic vs. transcendent in a cage match
to the death. they parceled the land into
checkerboard squares and i stood down,
a smiley face from head office was all it
took to buy my silence--needy much?
mummified compassion circuit much?
perfectly-preserved spock head piggy
bank found in dumpster--ebay here i
come! my cries of triumph echo off
the padded walls of the factory outlet
mall parking lot. never lose faith in the
parachute when you're halfway down.

Final Jeopardy

it's not the thought that counts; it's the 20 bucks.
don't know what hurt more: the lameness of the
lie or the bloody tomahawk on the pillow. and
baphomet graffiti rubber-stamped all over
duplex planet, colors fiercer closer to home
like a scab healing in reverse. roadkill on hot
tar like a kiss with fur stuck to it, and how the
dairy queen closing up for winter leaves me
hollow as a balloon. black cherry is the only
flavor dorothee ever liked, i wonder why.
and when she fell asleep just before they
caught the killer, i wondered about that too.
shrimp are high-tone but even pumpkin spice
cockroaches are just disgusting. miners die
in cave-ins, midges bang against the screen
door and the murderer hid every clue but
one. you're more likely to be killed by your
lover than by al-qaeda but that's not
important right now: with consummate
skill she fries onions she grew herself
in a flowerpot gord built for us, laughs,
says, 'final jeopardy.' i say, 'what?' the
world's mighty pistons freeze, prick
up their ears, wait for her answer.

Dancing Too Close

the sun slides below the horizon, valiantly pops
right back up, no, that's just me, stuck on fast-
forward again. i want mastodon for dinner, not
pizza pockets. the air fryer tries hard but isn't
fooling anyone. when i was a caveman every
star was an angry ghost, the space between
them a monster's reflection. ifrah left and not
even a power outage marked the disaster. me,
i grew a beard, spent a decade talking to trees.
jenneke said she hated seeing me waste my
potential: i said phobos orbits mars 3 times a
day, can you imagine? but, it dances too close,
keeps sinking lower, some day mars will just
rip her apart. when i finished my powerpoint
presentation she was gone, a domino's pizza
coupon standing in her place. kept a mormon
at the door for so long he begged for mercy,
ran away, said he was late for choir practice,
guess my soul's on its own. again. still. yet,
how truly swaddled in flame this highway is!
junk mail battalions thrum with commerce.
cavalcades of murmurations, a lucky free
spin. if i was in charge there'd be rubies
everywhere, and leaves would never fall.

Notes on an Explosion

explode is a word that deserves a lot more synonyms.
the honeysuckle throbs, the junk mail metastasizes,
the inbox is choked with equatorial liana vines.
dear tarzan, today i tied my shoes too fast, paid
the price with stiletto-shaped chest pains. but i
did kiss a girl while, on the screen above us, a
zombie battled a shark. her lips tasted like grape
kool-aid. the girl, not the shark. and the zombie
had no lips at all and was long past caring. the
dvd skips just before the graves are emptied.
a long tracking shot follows the footprints in
the sand that lead toward the mad doctor's
lab. i'm big on cracked ritual remembrance.
explode's not just a word; it's a whole vibe.
random detonations like gold dust, like
waking up in someone else's straitjacket,
digging a hole and having nothing to fill it
with. fed a bird who said he was a lizard,
before the egg cracks everything's up for
grabs. when my lover left for grad school
in halifax she made one last visit just to
change the sheets and beg me not to
fall apart so trust me on this: everything's
an explosion and everything's a song.

Slave to Fashion

my favorite jacket waited for my snores,
then grew legs and tiptoed out the door.
it left no note; i can only assume there
are limits to grace, that it hadn't signed
up for such self-abasing adventures. the
dizzying litanies of my failures surely
nauseated it as much as they did me.
faux-leather, it had a zip-away hood.
creased at the elbow from saluting my
inferiors, it danced with me when i
embarrassed myself on new year's eve,
listened to my boring stories, cheered
when i drew a perfect circle without
using a compass, kept a straight face
while i dreamed of being a rock star.
in 1986 i scored on my own net. now
my spaceship remains just a blueprint,
the zetan colony stillborn, the alien
parasite dying of boredom. my brain
used to shoot out thunderbolts: now
it's smaller than a walnut, no reason
to strut, to swagger–whatever we decide
about that impending extinction event,
every man should own one nice jacket.

Heavy Metal Super Center

the prisoner and the jailer breathe the same air,
the voter and the worm breathe the same air,
and spooky action at a distance works its magic
with a generosity that leaves me speechless.
mesons, leptons, all the quanta and qualia of a
hungover monday sing together, but did i get my
world-picture via diagrams or inheritance, and
would the world even recognize her reflection in
my world-picture? don't panic: this won't be on the
test. i swing my arms in harmony with my legs as if
this will trigger a greater harmony, a truce between
us and the mirror-world where down means up.
we abandoned the car at the base of the cn tower:
what's one mercury topaz, more or less, between
fellow carbon-based life forms? no edifying parable,
just some stuff that happened, like you and i just
happened, before uncoiling in disparate directions.
later on, the chess masters of jackson square threw
ketchup doritos at seagulls, sparking a feeding
frenzy of alarming savagery. how many nights i
traced your silhouette on the pillow, cataloged
lake erie's waves and never saw a duplicate. and what
would you say, if you were here, and muzak-version
guns n' roses was blaring in the produce aisle?

Short Trip

a desire is really a cry for help. your call is important
to us means something's wrong. before saturn ate
his children he said, you'd do the same to me if
you had the chance. every wrong number's a
world, every commuter's a galaxy. we're all paper
in holy books but get up off the couch too quickly
and see stars, burning clipper ships sinking on
the horizon. and eyes are windows it's true, but
so is everything else, and sifting universals from
particulars is no cheap trick when rush hour
makes you question your life choices, makes
you start passing on the right, on the gravel
shoulder. the dust cloud in the rearview
triggers the same guilty synapse that first-grade
detention did, life's such a short trip after all!
the atoms in my limbs and the atoms in my wishes
aren't on speaking terms but dorothee has a magic
book full of secret keys and switches: imagine
looking shame in the face and finding a fire escape,
a hero swinging from a rope ladder tied to the wing
of a cloud, a rainforest inside a teardrop. i scour
the dark corners and dead ends until all the
monks in the desert, arguing the grammar
of angel language, finally call it a day.

Monkey and the Monolith

banished from the campsite because the tribal chief
caught me fudging the numbers on the interstellar
motor scooter. escape velocity will not be mocked.
my god it's full of stars, is what the astronaut said
after his staring contest with the black hole. when
the monkey saw the monolith he learned about
desire and how to kill thy neighbour, that's why
we protect our passwords and rage at russian
bots like cartoon villains. lately we're either
being crushed with foam rubber anvils or
calling batman to complain about our
property tax increases. gerbils will run
in circles until the sun grows dim, the
president signs executive orders until
the carpal tunnel kicks in and he tags
in the stunt double. there's muted panic
cresting on the breeze, something about
rising lumber prices, levantine land grabs.
at times like this i used to call a friend
to calm me down--thanks for nothing,
caller i.d.! it sucks when you and your
body aren't on the same page anymore.
my fingers jitter so bad i can't even grip a
bowling ball without it turning into a pumpkin.

The Gravity of the Situation

the crown prosecutor twirls his mustache like
a monopoly-board banker. the sky pirouettes
in sync with the milky way's long lap around
everything that is. dorothee, baffled by her
notice of assessment, says, what happened
to freedom? crippled teeter-totter; emerald
ash borer infestation. time bends. flippers
strip victorian row houses down to the studs
while blasting led zeppelin 24/7. it feels like
a violation but my chessboard aldermen—
all pawns, no knights—are impassive as stone,
as the cosmic law telling the star, that facelift
isn't fooling anyone, joker, this is a one-way
trip. if you'd opened door number 3 in 1977
instead of sleeping in, you might be a captain
of industry by now, your tax loopholes
rechristened as acts of charity. if i was king
there'd be fewer cloudy days. dorothee could
retire, instead of battling blizzards on the
way to the punch clock. i pack her lunch the
night before, she spies a key-shaped cloud,
says this means our luck's about to change.
maybe i'll be stuck at a red and a wizard will
whisper the great secret right into my ear.
the planets will turn like bank vault tumblers
falling into place. dust bunnies and cobwebs
will find their own way out. all hail her dark

sorceries—this love stronger than death! while
she measures the honey for the tea i thank
the dealer who cut the cards. no doomsday
scenario #666 today, martin; today we're busy.

The Best Laid Plans

we worried about acid-washed jeans,
suddenly and fatally uncool after only
a semester, and sweat stains on the
dress shirt as misspent hours flowed
past like water under frozen rivers.
pin the tail on the anti-christ in the
church basement, nuclear winter
on prime-time specials, talking
ape astronauts from the future
foretelling our doom, doom, doom.
all those blue-ribbon facts we
memorized for a rainy day, now we're
baffled by a menu of counterproductive
choices when all we wanted was
cheerios and a high-speed chase.
the day after never came, now only
black friday deals excite us. there's
a 2 for 1 deal on spatulas tonight,
honey. check the online flyer, cash
in loyalty rewards points. these
fluorescent lights make me crazy,
crazy as mayonnaise pizza, crazy
as a million crazy crickets crying in
unison: attention walmart shoppers.

It's the Little Things

even monkeys hate mondays, says the father
as he ties his son to the altar. awful things
happened while i slept. nevertheless,
microbiota in my gut carry out their
grand plan, endlessly chomping.
butterflies and babies really know
the score. a cordillera of quilts
rises and falls as she dreams
her dad is laughing, and still
alive. the slash in the pumpkin
can't help but smile ironically,
the knife that put it there dreams
of being exhibit a in a very special
episode of perry mason. until
they call your name, read a
magazine, join the carnival.
another day is another day
farther away from the big
bang and closer to the finish
line, to downsizing, to giving
away the participation trophy
and clipping coffin coupons.
under the microscope even
an enemy looks like a brother.

T-Minus Whenever

my rocket ship is almost ready for blast-off—
goodbye, cruel world! re-zoning the
cherry orchard into a donut diner
was the last straw. i'll dodge the
ethereal scrap metal graveyard
that gives earth its unearned
halo, burn through space until
astronomers call me a star
and can you really blame me?
the forest is burning but we're
ok—our home entertainment
systems tell us so. when
we're out of lifeboats, we'll
do something. when we're
dead, we'll do something.
when we're hanging off the
volcano and the helicopter's
stuck in traffic, when piranhas
clog the crosswalks, when cops
kill jaywalkers but keep their
pensions and transhuman
billionaires gloat in their bunkers,
then we'll do something.
won't be long now.

Every Blade of Grass

a goblin stirred up dissension between body and soul;
another goblin made the bus driver miss my stop.
it hurts, kicking your way out of the egg, knowing
you're made out of the same stuff as bombs and
the senators who drop them. gutted pinata found
inside the large hadron collider, inherited incision
i use as a magic 8-ball, a way of charting the gap
between truth and news, angels and rockets.
maybe it doesn't hurt that bad, to be eaten by
a black hole, or to be a tortoise, even when the
vice-principal told my parents how hard it was
to coax me out of my shell. whose side was he
on? the mind recoils, the flesh records, you run
to the mirror for some cold gecko-eyed truth.
luckily tibor stops by; nothing brings him down.
tell him you had brain surgery, he'd say, i didn't
know you *had* a brain. dance, scarecrow, until
barton street leads to the emerald city. this is
oz if you want it. i never did pick a side, too busy
sailing across puddles, venerating every blade
of grass, cataloging, then alphabetizing, all the
ditches and culverts damned by unruly cherry
blossoms that reminded me of the scoops of
cherry ice cream i licked off dorothee's chest.

A Romantic Adventure

so sweet to be your man, instead of a strip of fly paper
or a studebaker chassis corroding in a lonely gully.

if this was a painting i'd call it 'crossroads' --our first
date in the rock garden with the fireflies gone berserk.

hello, members of the arthropod phyla, you were
witnesses. crickets hummed louder than niagara's

roar. it takes a dozen flavors of wind to make
the world spin, to fly a kite without losing it among

all the g5 radio towers. grace pierces the neural
net like a smile without a face. o to be the dollar

tree umbrella, trusty as a long-ago samurai,
that protects you from rain. o to be the cream.

Vampires in Literature

he wore an old blue suit
had a bushy beard and
neatly parted hair
with dandruff

he handed my library card
back to me and said, are
you aware you owe
$10.10 in fines?

uh...yeah...you mind if
i just pay it next time?

next time you'd better pay,
he said, leaning forward,
or your library privileges
will be REVOKED!

okay, next time i'll pay

i started to move away but
he grabbed my arm and said,
ahem! uh, excuse me....

what's the problem now?

ah ha, hah, i never know quite
how to bring this up, but i think
you and i could work out some
kind of a deal.

i jerked my arm away and said,
what're you talking about?

he looked around, made sure it
was safe, then said, i'll get right
to it. i might be able to shave a
few dollars off the money you
owe the library in exchange
for some of your blood

excuse me?

oh yes, i am quite serious

my blood? what do you want with it?

i want to drink it
he blushed a bit
i uh, just like the taste

also, i have found that in
some private matters
it gives me a bit of a boost
if you know what i mean

i stepped back and he said
please! my offer is genuine!

I ran away, looked for a manager,
bumped into a guy in the lobby
and said, do you know what that
psycho just said to me?

the guy looked where i was pointing
and said, oh, the blood guy? you
gonna do it?

what?

the guy shrugged and showed me
the strips of pinpricks running down
his arms. some of them looked
infected

the idea takes some getting used to,
he said, but for me it's worth it.
he takes the blood and my body
just makes more, right? and there's
a couple more dollars i get to keep!

i thought it over, then asked him,
why don't you just return your
library books on time, so you
don't have to pay any fines?

the guy just shook his head,
told me i just didn't get it

as i walked away i heard him call out,
if you ever have to pay any parking
tickets at the courthouse, look for
the woman with the red hair! she'll
give you the same deal!

Notes

The author wishes to thank CCENA (McMaster University's Center for Community-Engaged Narrative Arts) for their financial support,

And the editors of the following magazines, where some of these poems first appeared:

Exile
Queen's Quarterly
Hamilton Arts and Letters
Eunoia Review
Chiron Review
Nashwaak Review
Dollhouse Review

Milton Keynes UK
Ingram Content Group UK Ltd.
UKHW030940220724
445981UK00013B/562

www.quoir.com

Many voices. One message.

QUOIR

For more information about Darrell Epp,
or to contact him for speaking engagements,
please visit him on X @DarrellEpp.